spot

OUTDOOR FUN

CAMPING

by Nessa Black

AMICUS | AMICUS INK

tent

rain fly

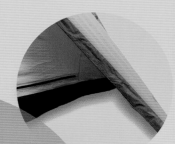

Look for these
words and pictures
as you read.

air mattress campfire

The car is all packed.
It's time to go camping.

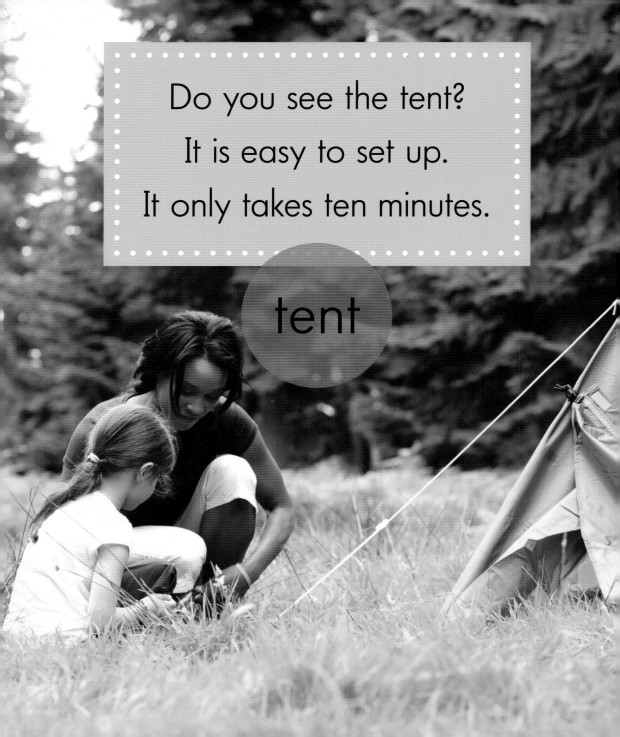

Do you see the tent?

It is easy to set up.

It only takes ten minutes.

tent

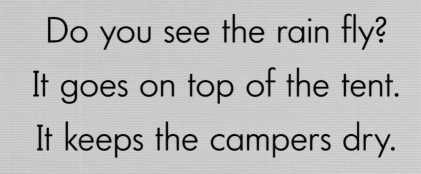

Do you see the rain fly?
It goes on top of the tent.
It keeps the campers dry.

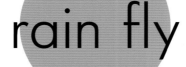

rain fly

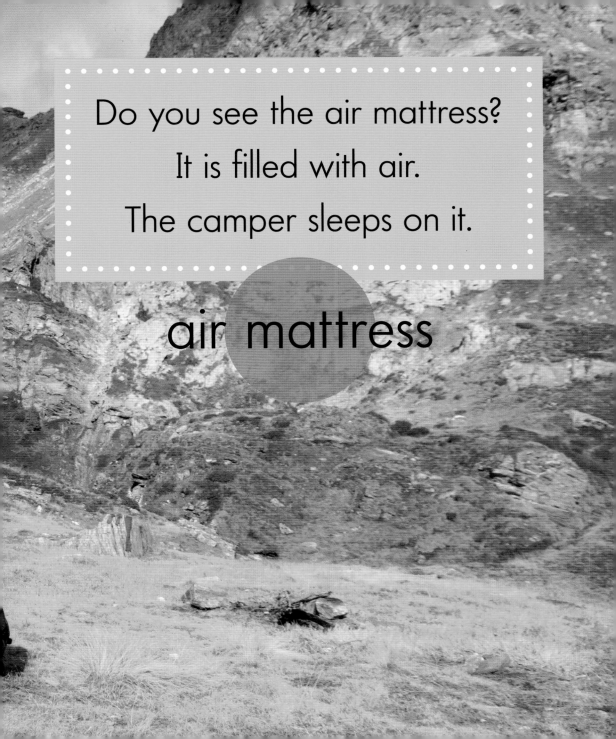

Do you see the air mattress?
It is filled with air.
The camper sleeps on it.

air mattress

Do you see the campfire?
Campers cook on it.
They roast marshmallows. Yum!

campfire

The campers go for a hike.
They see birds.

Wow! Look at all the stars. Camping is fun!

Do you see the tent?
It is easy to set up.
It only takes ten minutes.

tent

Do you see the rain fly?
It goes on top of the tent.
It keeps the campers dry.

rain fly

tent

rain fly

Did you find?

air mattress

campfire

Do you see the air mattress?
It is filled with air.
The camper sleeps on it.

air mattress

Do you see the campfire?
Campers cook on it.
They roast marshmallows. Yum!

campfire

spot

Spot is published by Amicus and Amicus Ink
P.O. Box 1329, Mankato, MN 56002
www.amicuspublishing.us

Library of Congress Cataloging-in-Publication Data
Names: Black, Nessa, author.
Title: Camping / by Nessa Black.
Description: Mankato, Minnesota : Amicus/Amicus Ink,
[2020] | Series: Spot outdoor fun | Audience: Grades:
K to Grade 3.
Identifiers: LCCN 2019003792 (print) | LCCN 2019014561
(ebook) | ISBN 9781681518480 (pdf) | ISBN
9781681518084 (library binding) | ISBN 9781681525365
(pbk.) | ISBN 9781681518480 (ebk.)
Subjects: LCSH: Camping--Juvenile literature. | Picture
puzzles--Juvenile literature.
Classification: LCC GV191.7 (ebook) | LCC GV191.7 .B55
2020 (print) | DDC 796.54--dc23
LC record available at https://lccn.loc.gov/2019003792

Printed in China

HC 10 9 8 7 6 5 4 3 2 1
PB 10 9 8 7 6 5 4 3 2 1

Wendy Dieker, editor
Deb Miner, series designer
Aubrey Harper, book designer
Shane Freed, photo researcher

Photos by Africa Studio/Shutterstock
cover, 16; sh22/iStock cover, 16;
lucentius/iStock cover 16; WesAbrams/
iStock 1; Youproduction/Shutterstock
3; Dean Mitchell/iStock 4–5; Givaga/
Alamy 6–7; Nesolenaya Alexandra/
Shutterstock 10–11; SanderStock/iStock
8–9; Hero Images Inc./Alamy 12–13;
anatoliy_gleb/Shutterstock 14–15

CAMPING